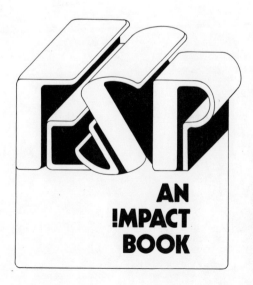

AN
!MPACT
BOOK

FRANKLIN WATTS | NEW YORK | LONDON

THOMAS G. AYLESWORTH

**ILLUSTRATED BY
GEORGE MacCLAIN**

Cover by Michael Horen

Library of Congress Cataloging in Publication Data

Aylesworth, Thomas G.
    ESP.

    (An Impact book)
    Bibliography: p.
    Includes index.
    SUMMARY: Briefly surveys the field of extra-
sensory perception with a description of experiments in the United States and other countries.
    1. Extrasensory perception — Juvenile litera-
ture. 2. Psychical research — Juvenile literature.
[1. Extrasensory perception. 2. Psychical research]
I. MacClain, George, ill. II. Title.
BF1321.A9   133.8   74-26797
ISBN 0-531-00826-6

CONTENTS

OTHER BOOKS
BY THE AUTHOR

The Alchemists: Magic into Science

Astrology and Foretelling the Future

Into the Mammal's World

It Works Like This

Monsters from the Movies

Mysteries from the Past

Servants of the Devil

Teaching for Thinking (with Gerald Reagan)

This Vital Air, This Vital Water

Traveling into Tomorrow

Vampires and Other Ghosts

Werewolves and Other Monsters

The World of Microbes

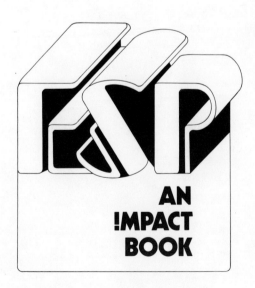

AN
!MPACT
BOOK

For Howard E. Smith, Jr.
Disbeliever, Friend, and
the Hero of the Preface

While I was working on this book, it seemed to me that everyone I met had some contribution to make. They would tell me about their own experiences in foretelling the future, visualizing what was happening in the present in a far place, or seemingly reading someone else's mind. Some of the stories were grim, some were humorous, and others were run-of-the-mill.

During that time also, something happened to me that can serve as an example of the kind of stories that my friends seemed to want to tell me. I was having lunch with an acquaintance when, for no reason at all, he asked me what I thought was a boring question. "What were your favorite books when you were little?"

Well, *Winnie-the-Pooh* had been a real treat for me, I guess. But it was read to me, so it didn't count. I had read the usual books that come in series — The Hardy Boys, The Black Stallion, and so on. But I didn't want to admit that.

Then, for some reason, the book that popped into my head was something called *Johnny Mouse and the Wishing Stick*. It was the first book that I had ever read all by myself, and I hadn't thought about it for years. Besides, I then re-

PREFACE

membered that it had been out of print for at least sixteen years and was not available in bookstores.

My friend thought that I was joking about the book. He had never heard of it.

We finished lunch, walked down the street, and went into a bookstore to snoop around. In the middle of a shelf in the juvenile section was a whole pile of *Johnny Mouse and the Wishing Stick* books. It turned out that they had just been delivered that day. And they had been put on the shelf while we were having lunch. The publisher had decided to bring them back into print after twenty years. My friend almost fainted, but he bought a copy of the book.

What is the purpose of telling you a dull story like that except to confess that I have had ESP experiences, too? I wanted to point out that most people have had something strange happen to them that cannot be explained away by calling them coincidences. And while these experiences may not be hair-raising, it is often the less dramatic ones that happen in normal, everyday life that make you sit up and take notice.

So keep an open mind, and, while you are about it, keep your eyes and ears open, too.

Thomas G. Aylesworth
Stamford, Connecticut

WHAT IS IT?

We receive information in many ways. We hear language and noises. We smell odors, both good and bad. We feel objects. We see things. And we taste substances. But there may be another way. This is the way of *ESP*.

ESP, or extrasensory perception, is a way of getting information without using any of what are thought of as our five common senses. It not only has nothing to do with these senses, but it also has no connection with the nervous system or the muscles. It is an area of study that is quite important today.

The study of ESP is part of the science called parapsychology. This is also called psychical research, or *psi*, for short. Besides ESP, there is another branch of psi communication, which includes the phenomenon in which an object seems to be moved by the mind alone. The mover does not touch the object and the object can be living or nonliving. This is called psychokinesis, or *PK*, for short. We will get to it in Chapter 8.

For the time being, let's stick to ESP. There are three accepted kinds, and they have been known for a long time. They are *clairvoyance, precognition*, and *telepathy*. Clairvoyance is the extrasensory perception of events that are taking place at the time of the perception. But the sensor cannot know about these events through any of the five senses. Precognition is the extrasensory perception of events in the future. Telepathy is the extrasensory perception of someone else's mental state.

There are some people who say that there are other kinds of ESP. Retrocognition — the extrasensory perception of past events — is one of these. But this is not accepted by students of ESP because there is no way of testing for it. The subject might actually have lived through the past event, or read about it, then told about it later. And there is no place in the serious study of ESP for messages from beyond the grave.

Reports of ESP experiences are many and varied. They are ancient, too. We have heard a lot about dreams of personal tragedies. There are stories about seeing the death of a relative or friend while sleeping. We hear about these happenings all the time. But stories like this were told long, long ago, too.

(5)

King Croesus of Lydia, in Asia Minor (reigned 560-546 B.C.), dreamed of the murder of his son. So he hired a guard to take care of the boy. Little did he know that the guard was the man in his dream who was supposed to kill the prince. You can believe that if you want to.

In 1858, Mark Twain and his brother Henry were working on separate boats on the Mississippi River. One night Mark Twain had a dream. He saw his brother lying in a metal coffin, dressed in one of Twain's own suits, with a bouquet on his chest. The bouquet had a red rose in the center.

A few days later, the boilers on Henry's boat exploded near Memphis. Mark Twain arrived in that city to find his brother in a metal coffin, dressed in one of Mark Twain's suits. Twain remembered his dream then. Suddenly an old lady came in with a bouquet and put it on Henry's chest. The bouquet had a red rose in the center.

Not all dreams of this type are precognitive. Some are clairvoyant or telepathic. And you don't have to be asleep and dreaming to have ESP. You can have flashes of insight during a daydream or while being fully awake. But there is also the matter of intuition. This is when you "just know" something and can't explain how you know.

Everyone has heard of cases in which, for example, a mother is playing bridge at a friend's house and suddenly feels uneasy. She gets up from the table, drives home, and finds her house on fire. There probably have been hundreds of cases in which the woman drives home and finds that her house is not on fire. But we cannot rule out the idea that, on occasion, ESP has been at work.

Suppose that the fire story is really a case of ESP. Did the woman get the message through clairvoyance? That is, did she get an impression of the event? Or was it telepathy? Could she have received a message from the mind of a person who was watching the fire?

There was a time, in more simple ages, when ESP was much more in favor than it is now. Suppose that you were able to convince your fellow citizens that you could know the future through precognition. Or see distant happenings through clairvoyance. Or read other people's minds through telepathy. You would be a powerful person in the community. You would be a prophet, a soothsayer, an oracle. Even today in some parts of the world, people are said to be able to find water by holding a stick in a certain way and walking over a field. These people, called *dowsers,* feel the stick tremble when they pass over underground water. Might this be a form of clairvoyance?

People have always thought that there was such a thing as luck. Do you know someone who always seems to be fortunate in games? Although most people think that luck cannot be explained, there are those who think that it might have something to do with psi. However, two psychologists at Emory University have found that students who believe in luck do not do as well in school as those students who do not believe in luck.

And what about religion? Most religious groups have had supernatural events as part of their beliefs. In fact, both types of psi — ESP and PK — are present in these religions. Prophecy is a type of precognition. Clairvoyance can be called revelation. Prayer could be considered a form of telepathy. And PK can be found in the miraculous answers to prayer.

PSI: MYTH
OR SCIENCE?

For centuries, stories about ESP sounded suspicious to those who had scientifically trained minds. After all, they were usually tales told *after* the fact. The event had already happened when the subject related having foretold it in a dream, for example. So it was impossible to test whether or not there was such a thing as ESP.

But one basic principle of science is that an idea should not be rejected just because it is hard to believe. We make mistakes sometimes, but a strange notion should be tested before it can be rejected. Besides, many of these psi stories came from sensible people.

The problem was, who was to study psi? The geologists, biologists, astronomers, chemists, and physicists were not equipped to do it. Their lines of work involve known and familiar properties of nature. So, for a long time, psi was considered to be merely a supernatural phenomenon. That meant that psi experiments were put on the shelf as far as scientists were concerned. Psi research did not get started for a very long time.

The investigations did not really get off the ground until the nineteenth century. Perhaps interest was piqued by some new discoveries in physics, such as universal fluids and interplanetary forces. These were upsetting enough to the scientific establishment. But then there was Franz Mesmer and his experiments with "mesmerism" — later to be called hypnotism. Hypnotism proved directly that people could influence each other without any kind of sensory contact.

In 1882, the Society for Psychical Research was founded in London. It was set up to investigate "mesmeric, psychical, and spiritualistic claims." Three years later came the American Society for Psychical Research in Boston.

The ASPR stated its purposes. It was concerned with:

The investigation of claims of telepathy, clairvoyance, precognition, retrocognition, veridical hallucinations and dreams, psychometry, dowsing, and other forms of paranormal cognition; of claims of paranormal physical phenomena such as telekinesis [psychokinesis or PK], materialization, levitation, and poltergeists; the study of

*automatic writing, trance speech, hypnotism, alterations
of personality, and other subconscious processes insofar
as they may be related to paranormal processes; in short,
all types of phenomena called parapsychological, psychic,
or paranormal.*

You can see that this group did not mention magic, astrology, witchcraft, or any type of occult practice.

Out of the investigations of mediums and communication with the spirit world came the consideration of thought transference from one person to another. Some people began to believe that the spirit medium might not be communicating with a spirit from another world. Rather, the medium might be picking up telepathic messages from a living person.

Slowly ESP and PK experimentation grew, even spreading to departments of psychology in great universities. During the first two decades of the twentieth century, much work went on at Harvard, Stanford, and the University of Groningen in the Netherlands. Courses in psi were offered at Bryn Mawr College, Smith College, and the University of Minnesota.

But these schools ran into trouble. Telepathy was a hard thing to work with. And psychology itself was still a new, suspicious-sounding study. Gradually the psi experiments were given up. However, some discoveries had been made. So, in a sense, the way was paved for future serious work.

The study of these phenomena began again at Duke University in North Carolina in 1927. William McDougall was a professor of psychology there, and he began his work studying psi. McDougall had been at Harvard and had been interested in ESP for years. He also had been a member of the Society for Psychical Research council.

Fortunately, the administration at Duke was more liberal than other administrations had been about psi, and McDougall was given more to work with than any psychologist had ever been able to afford. So when he set up his laboratory, psychical research had turned the corner and now could be called parapsychology. *Para* in Greek means "alongside," so *parapsychology* means "equal to the science of psychology." McDougall decided to devote his laboratory to the study of telepathy, clairvoyance, precognition, and psychokinesis. He was not looking for ghosts. He was looking for psi abilities in human beings.

McDougall brought two biologists to Duke, J. B. and Louisa E. Rhine, a married couple who had been experimenting in the field of psi at Harvard. The Rhines' chief interest at the time was not telepathy, but the question of survival after death. They had been studying mediums and their communication with the dead. But they soon realized that this was not getting them very far. They had been able to put a medium in one room and a subject in another and achieve some thought transference. But they still could not figure out where the medium was getting the information. Was it coming from a dead person or from the other room? They decided to stick with the idea that telepathy was the source of the information.

In 1934, the Duke laboratory came out with its first report, called *Extrasensory Perception,* which described the Rhines' early work. In their experiments, the Rhines had relied heavily on Zener cards, which consist of twenty-five cards to the deck, with five identical cards each in five different "suits." The suits consist of five cards marked with crosses, five cards marked with circles, five cards marked with stars, five cards marked with squares, and five cards marked with wavy lines.

One experiment involves shuffling and cutting the cards so that they are all mixed up. Then the subject is asked to name, one by one, the card on the top of the deck — before it is turned over. You can see that the subject has only one chance in five of guessing the card by luck. So he or she should guess only five out of the whole deck. If a large number of test runs are made, and the subject gets many more than five right per run, then it is felt that the person has ESP powers.

Hubert Pearce, a divinity student at Duke, had volunteered to be the subject of one of the Rhines' experiments. The pile of twenty-five cards was placed face down on a table. Pearce named correctly each card in the order in which it was stacked!

Twenty-five out of twenty-five! The odds against being able to do that by chance are 298,023,223,876,953,125 to 1. Pearce, however, was never able to do it again.

Throughout their research and experimentations, the Rhines faced many problems. A major difficulty was that almost none of the work that had been done before had been done scientifically. No one had set up an experiment in which the variables were sufficiently controlled to determine whether telepathy or clairvoyance was being exercised.

For example, take the case of two people in separate rooms. One of them looks at a card, and the other names a card. Was a telepathic message sent from one mind to the other? Or did the receiver visualize the card by clairvoyance?

There was another problem in the early days of psi experimentation. It was difficult to pin down psi experiences because the subject thought that he or she was being acted upon by an outside force. Now the research tends to indicate that the force is *within* the subject. That makes it easier to test, since you are dealing only with one individual.

The psi process can now be thought of as having two parts. In the first part, an item of information is received unconsciously. How this happens is not known. In part two, the selected item is taken in on a conscious level. It is here that psi experiments have been forced to operate. It is, so far, impossible to test the unconscious receivers. We don't know where or who they are, much less how they operate. And besides, it is hard enough testing conscious receivers.

**WHO HAS
THE POWER?**

Long ago it was believed that only special people had ESP power. But now it is felt by parapsychologists that almost everyone may have it to a certain extent. Who are these people who actively and consciously possess this ability, and when do they have it? These are difficult questions to answer because of the differences among people.

First of all, those people who do not believe in ESP are poorer subjects than those who do. Tests have shown that other poor subjects are withdrawn children, defensive people, psychotherapy patients who have just had a poor session with their analysts, and students who dislike their teacher.

In the case of students who disliked their teacher, when that teacher was giving ESP tests, the students scored lower than random chance. But when the same students were given the test by a well-liked teacher, they scored better than random chance.

Sometimes even good subjects have bad days. As in normal behavior, the psi subjects tend to lose skills when they are under stress. Actually, there are cases of "psi-missing." In these instances, the subject who is normally very sensitive scores lower on the tests than would be the case in pure guesswork. That's what anxiety can do.

This fact has been expanded to cover another experiment. In this one, the "sheep" and the "goats" were really separated.

The "sheep" — those who believe in ESP — tend to score higher than random chance. But the "goats" — those who oppose ESP — generally score lower than random chance. It has been said that they are under stress to disprove ESP and so are a type of "psi-missing" person. However, tests were made and it was found that the goats were not consciously trying to miss. It was all unconscious.

Who has the power? It seems that there is no way of telling. The Rhines have found people with ESP power who range in age from four to sixty. However, it seems that the younger a person is, within limits, of course, the better subject he or she is.

Academic abilities don't have much to do with it, either. Duke students with high grades, when tested by the Rhines, had no more ESP power than those with low grades. Retarded children as a group have been tested and they exhibit, on average, the same ability in ESP as normal children as a group.

There seems to be no difference between men and women in their abilities. But people who are confident seem to do much better. However, lose your confidence and your ESP scores go down. This is similar to an athlete having a bad day. Sometimes the ball just won't go through the basket.

Concentration is important. One subject at Duke suffered on his scores when his hometown girl friend came for a visit. Another did poorly when he heard that there was an illness in the family. Catching colds made several people fall off in their guesswork.

One of the strangest factors may be the moon. When he heard of a report from Russian scientists that indicated that ESP performances improved when there was a full moon, Dr. Stanley Krippner, a parapsychologist, went back over some of his own research. He confirmed that the full moon seemed to have had some effect on the ESP subject's accuracy.

Dr. Arthur Guirdhan, an English psychologist, has studied people with strong psi abilities and looked at their medical histories. He was able to dispel the common argument that people with psi abilities are often hysterical. He found a few, but due to unusual occurrences they were entitled to be hysterical.

One of them was the wife of a British sailor. She had had a history of being precognitive. One night she dreamed of her husband's ship being torpedoed. When she told her neighbors of her fear, they were hostile and suspicious. Later, her husband's ship was torpedoed. Guirdhan noted, "Under such circumstances, an anguished patient can be forgiven for a few hysterical symptoms."

Some people have argued that the person with high psi ability could be the victim of delusions. But Guirdhan points out that people who suffer from delusions are usually guarded, hostile, and suspicious. No suspicious psychic could be successful, nor could a guarded one. ESP ability involves the ability to communicate.

So much for the descriptions of who has psi ability — at least human psi ability. Other animals may have it too. Actually, there was a group that branched off at Duke University during the 1950s that studied animal parapsychology — the "anpsi" group. They tested cats, dogs, and pigeons. At the same time, researchers in France were studying rodents. But more of that later.

**THE WORLD
OF DREAMS**

In the middle of the 1940s, a new idea was born. It was thought that the three types of ESP were just different examples of the same thing. From that premise came an attempt to relate parapsychology to the other sciences — physics, biology, and psychology.

Let's take physics, which is the study of the physical. ESP has yet to be explained in physical terms, so physicists cannot account for it. But why is psi nonphysical? For one thing, it does not depend on time. If there is such a thing as precognition, time is not a factor. For another, as in telepathy and clairvoyance, psi does not depend on distance.

However, there is another side of the coin. PK, if it does exist, is a type of energy. And physicists study energy. In the past, new elements, new planets, and other physical things have been discovered when scientists found physical phenomena consisting of the gravitational pull on one object by another undiscovered object. The problem was checked out and the unknown object was found. Could this happen with PK?

Biologists and psychologists also must go to work on the problem. There may be some form of mental energy in psi which we have not yet discovered.

In the field of psychology, there were those psychologists, such as William McDougall, William James, and Sigmund Freud, who thought that the study of ESP was a part of their discipline. After all, part of psychology is the study of the unconscious mind.

In the last two or three decades, researchers started to experiment with the unconscious mind, mainly by working with sleeping people in dream laboratories. To understand their work, we need to know a little bit about how we sleep. Here's what happens to you.

You are drowsy, lying in bed waiting for sleep to come. Your eyes are closed and your pulse and breathing are steady. Your temperature is slowly dropping. Your brain waves show what is called an *alpha rhythm,* with a frequency of about nine waves per second. This is the threshold of sleep.

From time to time, a sudden jerk of the body may wake you up for part of a second, but you immediately slip back toward sleep. Some people sleep with their eyes partially open. But at this point, they don't see anything.

Next comes stage 1 of sleep. The voltage of the brain is now quite low. The muscles are more relaxed and the heartbeat slows down.

Stage 2 is next. There are rapid brain waves and a pattern of slow eye movements — sort of a rolling of the eyes from side to side. If you were to be awakened during stage 2, you would say that you had not been asleep at all. But you probably would have been out for about ten minutes.

About half an hour later, stage 3 arrives. The brain waves are bigger and more spread out. Everything is completely relaxed — even breathing. Heartbeat, temperature, and blood pressure are down. It takes a loud noise to wake you.

Finally, there is stage 4. Even loud noises will seldom awaken you when you are in this stage. Usually, most of the first half of the night is spent in stage 4 sleep, especially if you are tired. This is the most necessary time of sleep if you want to feel rested in the morning.

After stage 4, the process reverses. You gradually drift from stage 4 to stage 3 to stage 2. But when you begin to exhibit the physical symptoms of stage 1 again, it is a little different from when you were awake first going to sleep. It would take a loud noise to awaken you in this stage 1.

Your eyes start making rapid, darting movements, as if you were looking at something. These are the same rapid eye movements, or REM's, that you exhibit when you look at a movie or a TV show. What is happening? You are following the action of a dream. Your heart beats faster and your blood pressure goes up. But your muscles are relaxed and your body is still.

If you were to be awakened at this point, you would be able to describe your dream. But if you are not awakened, you might never remember any part of it.

After the dream, you will probably drift back into stage 4 again. In another hour and a half, it is time to dream again. This sequence can be repeated four or five times before you actually wake up.

Dreams have always fascinated people and scientists are

no exception. Much work has been done on this subject since the invention of a machine for detecting brain waves and recording them on an electroencephalogram, or EEG. And it can also be used to monitor the activity of the brain during sleep.

It was with this device that the different levels of sleep and the period of REM's were found. But do all of us have those rapid eye movements? Dr. Ian Oswald, of the University of Edinburgh, Scotland, tested blind people. He found that those who had been blind since birth did not move their eyes during their dream periods. Not being able to see, they had never learned to do this. People who became blind later in life did move their eyes. They had not lost the habit. This was further proof of the connection between REM's and dreaming.

By the way, research has indicated that 82.7 percent of our dreams are in color.

The EEG can be used in psi experimentation even when the subject is awake. For example, Lalsingh Harribance, a man from Trinidad, claimed that he could describe a person's appearance and personality by concentrating on that person's hidden photograph. Dr. Robert Morris of the Psychical Research Foundation in Durham, North Carolina, tested him. Harribance was to concentrate on the hidden photos and tell whether the pictures were of men or women.

By using an EEG, Morris found that Harribance's brain waves showed a high percentage of alpha waves. High alpha wave readings usually mean that the subject is relaxing and concentrating. The best psi results usually occur when the subject goes from low to high alpha wave patterns. That's when the person shifts from an active state to a passive state. Harribance's results were much better than chance.

On Friday, July 20, 1973, a young woman in Brooklyn, New York, dreamed that she had seen an acquaintance looking at a picture of a collapsed building. The picture, she said, was on the front page of the New York *Daily News*.

On August 3, the Broadway Central Hotel in New York did collapse, and the *News* printed the picture on the front page. It was the same picture the woman had described.

The interesting thing about this story is that she had described her dream more than a week before to researchers at the Maimonides Medical Center's Division of Parapsychology and Psychophysics. This Brooklyn institution, until 1972, specialized in studies of the effects of hypnosis on ESP. That year they received a grant of $52,000 from the National Institute of Mental Health to study dreams.

The Maimonides Dream Laboratory has been in operation since 1963 and is particularly active at night. It is then that subjects come in to sleep and have their dreams monitored. These people are paid fifty dollars to sleep for five straight nights. Six of them are used per week.

On the first night, one of the researchers tries to send a telepathic message to the subject. It is a message about one of six different pictures. The next morning, the subject is shown the six pictures. If the subject picks the target picture in the first three choices, he or she is accepted for testing. About half the people pass this test.

On two of the other four nights, the subject watches a short film. Then he or she goes to sleep. A researcher is monitoring the brain waves and eye movements of the sleeping person. An EEG tells the researcher when the subject is dreaming. The subject is wakened after each dream to give a report on whether or not the film has affected his or her dreams.

On the other two nights, another person sees a film. While the first subject is sleeping, the person who saw the film tries to send telepathic messages about the film to the subject. Again the subject is awakened after each dream to give a report.

Dr. Charles Honorton of Maimonides says that 65 percent of spontaneous ESP events are the result of dreams. In his experiments, he would let the receiving subjects go to sleep. When their brain waves hit the high alpha wave level, sending subjects would try to concentrate on art prints. The senders were placed in distant rooms or sometimes in other buildings. The sleeping subjects, who were having a period of high REM's, were then awakened and reported their dreams. About seven out of ten seemed to have been getting the message of the art prints.

VISIONS OF
THE PRESENT

A woman going on a business trip packed her dresses in a trunk and checked the trunk at the railroad station. The trunk was to accompany her on a train trip. She got on the train in New York, but when she arrived at her destination, the trunk was not there. Everybody looked for it, but without success.

The woman checked into her hotel thinking that she would have to purchase new clothes the next day.

But that night she had a dream. She saw her trunk covered with snow on an isolated part of the station platform. There was no claim check on it.

The next morning she called the man at the station who had led the search for the trunk. When she finished describing her dream, he laughed at her. "Well, young lady," he said, "we don't find trunks by dreams."

The woman told him, "You don't find trunks anyway. Suit yourself, and the company can put up $1,000 in cash." He looked, and the trunk was found — covered with snow and on the isolated part of the platform that the woman had described from her dream.

Or take the case of the wife of a nineteenth-century British general. She wrote: "On September 9, 1848, at the siege of Mooltan, my husband, Major-General Richardson, C.B., then adjutant of his regiment, was most severely and dangerously wounded, and supposing himself dying, asked one of the officers with him to take the ring off his finger and send it to his wife, who at that time was fully 150 miles distant, at Ferozepore. On the night of September 9, 1848, I was lying in my bed, between sleeping and waking, when I distinctly saw my husband being carried off the field, seriously wounded, and heard his voice saying, 'Take this ring off my finger, and send it to my wife.' All the next day I could not get the sight or the voice out of my mind. In due time I heard of General Richardson having been severely wounded in the assault on Mooltan. He survived, however, and is still living. It was not for some time after the siege that I heard from Colonel L., the officer who helped to carry General Richardson off the field, that the request as to the ring was actually made to him, just as I had heard it at Ferozepore at that very time."

Famous people have had clairvoyant experiences, too. Giuseppe Garibaldi, the founder of modern Italy, was at sea. He had a dream that a group of people were carrying his mother's body to her grave. It later turned out that the day he had the dream was the day that his mother had died. Some other well-known people who had clairvoyant dreams were Percy Shelley, the poet; Victor Hugo, the writer; Sir Arthur Conan Doyle, the creator of Sherlock Holmes; Thomas Edison, the inventor; and Upton Sinclair, the novelist.

Now picture this. It happened in 1965. A woman student at the University of California at San Francisco lay on a laboratory bed. She was hooked up to various machines. There was an electroencephalograph connected to her head surface. There was a machine to measure her galvanic skin response by recording her skin temperature and moisture. And there was a REM (rapid eye movement) indicator. Add to that machines to record her blood pressure and heartbeat rate. The wires from these machines ran through a wall into a laboratory room next door.

She was asleep, having occasional five- and ten-minute dreams. But suddenly something happened to her EEG readings. Alpha waves began to appear. Everything else remained normal.

On a shelf, six feet over her head, a card with a five-digit number on it had been placed. The number had been picked at random from a box full of cards with numbers on them. Even Dr. Charles Tart, the scientist in charge of the experiment, did not know what the number was. But the girl, when she came out of her sleep, did. She called out the number — 35123. That was correct.

Let's take one more example to illustrate a point. A Canadian sawmill owner from time to time spent the night at his logging camp with his lumberjacks. One night while he was in camp he lost his wallet. Weeks later he had a dream.

In his dream, he saw his wallet at the bottom of the well at the camp. The next day he made a special trip to the camp, found the wallet at the bottom of the well, and drove back home.

This story illustrates the point that a message does not necessarily have to be sent by a second person in order for clairvoyance to occur. But for some reason, this was not realized for some time. There were stories of people who were at the grocery store, felt a signal, and ran home to find a loved one in serious trouble. We assumed that the person in trouble was sending a message. We forgot that the receiver was more important than the sender.

In the early 1930s, the Duke laboratory researchers were concentrating on telepathy experiments, but they switched to clairvoyance for a very good reason. It was difficult to plan telepathy experiments.

It may sound easy to organize a simple telepathy experiment. But suppose that the sender merely thinks of a card. He does not have the physical card in his possession but he must write down his choice. If the receiver guesses the card, is it telepathy or clairvoyance? Did the receiver get a message from the sender or from the sender's written record?

So it was decided to switch from telepathy to clairvoyance where the controlled experiment was easier to set up. All that had to be done was to guess concealed cards. No one knew what the cards were, so there could be no telepathy involved. This had been tried before by Charles Richet in the 1870s.

When the 1934 Duke laboratory report, mentioned before, came out, it told that there had been a great deal of success with clairvoyance experiments. In one experiment, the subject was put in a building one hundred yards away from the building in which the experimenter handled the target cards. The target cards were dealt out, face down, at a rate of one per minute. After twenty-five of them had been dealt, they were examined and their order was written down.

But the subject had been recording his selections one by one as he guessed them. So he had made all his guesses before the experimenter knew the order of the cards.

Experiments such as this came in series. The subject would go through two sets of twenty-five cards per day for six days. The results were amazing. Pure chance, it was figured, would give sixty hits out of the three hundred chances. But there were people who came up with 119 hits. And the chances of that happening by accident are millions to one.

You might think that the 1934 report would have set the scientific community on its head. But not so. In the beginning, there were scientists who were rather open-minded. There were also a few who were friendly toward these new ideas. In fact, many other psychologists tried to repeat the Duke experiments.

The problem was that these scientists were not as highly trained as the Duke group, and they had little experience. So, many of them failed in their experiments and began to say that the Duke work was not scientific. These failures were reported and the press and radio people had a field day. The popular publicity did not sit well with established psychologists and they began to publish attacks on the Rhines and their co-workers. The attacks continued from about 1937 to 1940 and then seemed to stop.

Meanwhile, the believers had, so far as they were concerned, proved the existence of clairvoyance. What was to be next? Telepathy was waiting. But there were still problems in separating telepathy from clairvoyance. So it was decided to let telepathy wait and go on to precognition.

By the way, even today not all people are pleased by the clairvoyant. In 1973, the Securities and Exchange Commission of the United States federal government told the psychic Joseph DeLouise to stop making predictions about the stock market. They warned him that he could be fined $10,000 or put in jail for two years, or both. The SEC claimed that DeLouise had violated the 1940 Investment Advisors Act. But DeLouise felt that he had a constitutional right to express his clairvoyant feelings.

In all fairness, the SEC was right. Whether or not DeLouise had precognitive powers, those who believed in him would buy or sell as he told them to. This could force the stocks up or down. He would have been influencing the market.

ESP

**VISIONS OF
THE FUTURE**

It has been said that about 10 percent of adult Americans have, at some time in their lives, gone on a precognition trip into the future. What happened was that they dreamed something was going to happen and it did.

Probably one of the most famous cases was the story told by Abraham Lincoln. He was at a White House party celebrating the surrender of General Robert E. Lee. Lincoln was moody. He finally explained his depression. It seemed that he had had a dream. He had heard muffled sobs in his dream and had left his bed to go to the lower floor of the White House.

"I kept on until I finally arrived in the East Room," he said. ". . . Before me was a catafalque on which rested a corpse in funeral vestments. Around it were stationed soldiers and there was a throng of people, some gazing mournfully upon the corpse, whose face was covered, and some weeping pitifully.

" 'Who is dead in the White House?' I demanded of one of the soldiers.

" 'The President,' was his answer. 'He was killed by an assassin.' "

Early in 1973, an Associated Press story by Will Grimsley told of some examples of precognition in the family of baseball star Roberto Clemente, who was killed in an airplane crash while he was taking relief supplies to the survivors of an earthquake in Managua, Nicaragua. These premonitions, which were told to the reporter by Vera Christiana Clemente, the ballplayer's widow, occurred before the great Pittsburgh Pirate outfielder left on the plane flight from which he never returned.

Roberto, Jr., age seven, told his grandmother, "Daddy is leaving for Nicaragua, but he is not coming back." Clemente's father said, "I had this terrible dream. I saw the plane crash and Roberto go down with it."

Premonition tales are common. For example, an Ohio woman was in church one Sunday and her automobile was stolen. Two nights later her daughter dreamed that the car was at a certain place in downtown Cleveland. The daughter told her husband and the two of them drove to the spot. There was the car. That sounds like clairvoyance. But, as it happened, people at the scene said that the car had been parked there for only a few minutes before the couple arrived. The dream was a dream of the future, not the present.

It was long thought that precognition messages were almost always urgent. They told of death and disease, money and happiness. Now we know that messages are often received about other things as well as about catastrophes and strokes of fortune.

Louisa Rhine made a study of the subject matter of ESP dreams. One-third of them were clairvoyant in nature and the other two-thirds were precognitive. Part of the reason for her study was to see if the receiver was the one to select the message that was to be received. It would be guessed, if most of the dreams were crisis types, that the sender was the one who was more important than the receiver. If the messages were run-of-the-mill, the receiver was the one who selected them, and thus more important than the sender.

Emotional relationships are important when one is studying dreams, so the cases were divided up based upon the identity of the person seen in the dream. There were four groups. The first one consisted of dreams in which the dreamer was the star of the show, with few other people involved. An example of this was a girl who dreamed that she was in a drive-in movie theater. She turned and saw a man in a cowboy hat take a drink from a bottle. Days later she was really in a drive-in movie theater and did see the man drink. But obviously the dreamer was the important character in this dream.

The second group contained dreams of the subject's immediate family. The third group contained the dreamer's other relatives — aunts, uncles, grandparents, in-laws — and neighbors, friends, and even pets. Finally, the fourth group contained people that the dreamer had never met, although the subject may have heard of them.

These four groups were then divided up into crisis cases and noncrisis cases. Crisis cases contained death, accidents, illnesses, medical operations, and weddings. The noncrisis cases were subdivided into two types — important and unimportant. Here is the score out of 2,878 dreams:

Relationship	% crisis cases		% noncrisis cases	Total %
		Important	Unimportant	
Self	7	17	9	33
Family	27	10	2	39
Distant Relative	10	4	1	15
Strangers	6	4	3	13
Total %	50	35	15	100

Notice that only half the dreams were crisis cases. Notice also that 15 percent of the dreams were trivial. And 13 percent were about strangers. So it would appear that the urgency of an event is not the main reason for ESP dreams.

One case history collected by Louisa Rhine concerns a young mother in the state of Washington. A horrible dream had awakened her. In the dream, a large chandelier had fallen and had crushed her baby. She saw the smashed crib in her dream and noticed that the clock in the room stood at 4:35 A.M. Outside the house the wind was blowing and a heavy rain was falling.

The mother woke up, ran to the baby's room, and took the child back to the master bedroom. She also noticed that the weather was pleasant outdoors, unlike the weather in her dream. She told her dream to her husband and they went back to sleep. Two hours later, all three people were awakened by a crash. Sure enough, the chandelier in the baby's room had fallen and crushed the crib. The wind was blowing, the rain was falling, and the clock in the nursery stood at 4:35 A.M.

There have been other types of precognition tests. In one experiment, the subject is supposed to guess which of four lamps will light next. The lamp that will light is chosen in a completely random way. Much success has been realized in this type of testing. The subjects are more apt to guess the correct lamp when they are happy than when they are sad.

But humans may not have a corner on precognition. Dr. Helmut Schmidt has worked with mice. He used an electric coin flipper for his experiments. The chances are fifty-fifty that the head of the coin will come up and the same, of course, that the tail will come up on the coin. The mice were placed in an electrically wired cage with two compartments in it. The coin was flipped to decide which of the compartments would be shocked.

If the mouse had precognition, it would be able to move to the compartment that was not going to carry the electrical shock. In the cases where the mouse moved after the coin toss and before the shock — and there were more than three thousand of these cases — the mice got the electricity only 47 percent of the time. This is a significantly better rate than the expected 50 percent of the time.

A California boy seemed to have an unusual amount of telepathic rapport with his uncle. The uncle lived a long distance away, but came to visit the boy and his family as often as he could.

There is nothing odd about this, of course. But the strange part is that the uncle never told the family when he would drop in, yet he was always expected. Somehow, each time that the uncle was about to arrive, the boy would get a "message" and tell his family, "Uncle Jimmy is coming to see us." Within a few hours, the uncle would show up.

Years later, the uncle was killed in a car crash in France. On the very day that this happened, the boy was found in a trancelike state by his mother. She asked him what was wrong. He told her that Uncle Jimmy was dead. It wasn't until two days later that the family got the official news.

It was this kind of happening that the Duke group finally decided to study. Five members of the laboratory got together in the mid-1940s and laid out their scientific plans. They were going to put the sender and the receiver in different rooms. The sender had a deck of Zener cards which he looked at, one by one.

Next the receiver was to name the symbol on the card that the sender was looking at. Each session contained four runs of the twenty-five cards. Then the sender would check the number of hits. Only this number was recorded. But the percentage of hits was high enough to indicate that there is a strong case to be made for the existence of telepathy. The sender's messages apparently were received in the same way that the uncle communicated to his nephew.

There had been one problem in the investigation of telepathy, however. Beginning in 1934, Dr. S. G. Soal, an English mathematician at London University, had tried to repeat some of the Rhines' early work in telepathy. He went at it until 1939 and finally had to admit that he had had no success with it at all. He had used 160 subjects and the whole thing had been a failure. It was because of results such as this that people had rejected the 1934 Duke report.

But later, one of Soal's colleagues, Whately Carington,

said that he should have looked for the "displacement effect." Perhaps correct guesses had been made just before or just after the target card. Soal found that two of his subjects had been amazingly able to guess the card that immediately followed the target card.

Some cases of telepathy have been studied in which the receivers seem to be practicing object reading. This is sometimes called psychometry or psychoscopy. W. H. C. Tenhaeff, director of the Parapsychology Institute at the University of Utrecht, the Netherlands, performed an experiment, or rather a series of experiments, in this area.

His subject, a woman, was handed an envelope that contained a picture of a man. The man was a personal friend of Tenhaeff. She reached in the envelope and touched the photograph without looking at it. This photograph was the inductor, or the ESP impression article. The woman then began to describe the man in the photograph.

"Someone who reads and writes a lot. He is at home in any field. He performs journalistic work. He is quickly stimulated. He leads a hurried and irregular life. I see him writing while seated on a train. He picks up every scrap of news. This is not just curiosity — he has to keep abreast of everything that happens. He can be curt at times. Stacks of paper lie on his desk in a complete jumble. He has a good sense of humor. He speaks foreign languages. Machines form part of his environment. I hear a regular thumping sound. The air reeks. I smell a peculiar, vile scent. The uproar is awful. He himself does not work among the machines, but he walks between them. He sits at a desk. He has a feeling for poetry. He gets a lot of books sent to him."

The man in the photograph was the managing editor of a newspaper. He did have a jumbled desk. His office was next to the noisy composing room that smelled of printer's ink. Everything else that she said about him was accurate.

Tenhaeff decided that she was reading his thoughts about his friend by telepathy. There was no proof that the photograph was helping the woman. Perhaps it was just making Tenhaeff's thoughts stronger. It stimulated his thinking about his friend and his thoughts may have been enforced upon his subject.

Commander Edgar Mitchell, who was the lunar module pilot on the Apollo 14 space shot in 1971, set up some telepathic experiments to be performed during that flight. He tried some telepathic communications with four "sensitive" people on earth. Later, he wrote a scientific paper describing the results of that test as statistically significant.

"During the Apollo 14 lunar expedition, I performed an extrasensory perception experiment — the world's first in space. In it five symbols — a star, cross, circle, wavy line, and square — were oriented randomly in columns of twenty-five. Four persons in the United States attempted to guess the order of the symbols. They were able to do this with success that could be duplicated by chance in one out of three thousand experiments. This in parapsychology experiments is considered reasonably successful."

In 1972, he announced that he was going to set up a firm in Houston to study "the psychic potential of man and other forms of life." Mitchell thought that this would "help people to develop greater relationship to other people and to the processes of nature."

It might be proper here to ask how a scientifically trained person such as Mitchell came around to a belief in ESP. Here is his explanation.

"When I first began looking at psychic phenomena in 1967, I was quite skeptical. I had spent years learning the objective methods of science, and along the way I had unconsciously picked up the negative attitude toward psychic research that is unfortunately common among scientists who do not know much about it. But to my surprise, the high quality of the research made it impossible for me — on the very grounds of scientific method and objectivity — to disbelieve the validity of the findings and their implications for civilization."

MOVING
OBJECTS

Psychokinesis, or PK, is a parallel study that may belong with ESP in psi. It is the movement of objects by means of mind power — without touching the objects.

In the 1930s, an Englishman, Harry Price, experimented with PK. His subject was a young girl. She was to try to depress a telegraph key without touching it. The key was hooked up with an electrical circuit in such a way that a light bulb would come on if the key were moved far enough. Price added some controls to the experiment to make sure the girl did not touch the apparatus. He blew a soap and glycerin bubble over the apparatus and placed a glass cover over the setup. Then he put a wire cage over the whole thing.

The girl caused the light to come on several times. And at the end of the experiment the bubble had not been broken.

From very early times, continuing through to the present, it has been the belief of many gamblers that they can exercise PK. Many of them think that they can make the dice fall right by talking to them. Others believe that they can get good cards by concentrating. Still others are sure that they can make the roulette ball fall where they want. And there are reputable researchers who consider a fair game of chance to be a contest between people out to prove whose PK abilities are the greatest.

Early in the 1930s, the people at Duke University began to test PK. It started like this. They had been studying clairvoyance. They already knew that the distance between the experimenter and the subject didn't seem to make any difference as far as hits were concerned. So they decided that if space did not affect clairvoyance, time might not affect precognition. They went on to test this.

In December of 1933 a subject who had been very good at clairvoyance was brought back to the laboratory. There he was asked to predict the order of cards in a pack. But this was done before the cards were shuffled. He was also asked to tell the order of the cards in a pack after they were shuffled. His scores on the two types of guessing were about the same.

Then a question came up. Could the order of the cards have been affected by some kind of psi, since they were shuffled by human hands? A mechanical shuffler was built. Actually, no one in the lab at that time thought that psi could control the order of the cards when they were shuffled by hand. But to eliminate all doubt, as good scientists should, they used their automatic shuffler.

The results of the mechanical shuffling were about the same as the results from hand shuffling. But then trouble arrived from an unexpected source.

One of the Duke researchers thought that he might be influencing the order of the test cards in the shuffling machine by concentration. If he were unconsciously using PK, he was ruining the precognition experiments. If a person could control the shuffling of the cards, he or she might have some knowledge of their order. And when the subject predicted the order of the cards, how could it be said that this was an example of precognition? It could also be a telepathic message sent out by the researcher.

Rhine and his colleagues began to test PK by using dice. In the beginning, the subjects tried to throw two dice so that their sum was greater than seven. Fifteen out of a possible thirty-six combinations of two dice are greater than seven. So, out of the 6,744 throws that they made, 2,810 would be expected to total more than seven. But they hit it 3,110 times, which was a billion-to-one chance.

But now, the scientists reasoned, what if the subjects were predicting the roll unconsciously? That would mean that they were using precognition to guess the number instead of PK to control the dice. What a mess.

The PK tests were then tightened up. The pair of dice was released mechanically and allowed to roll down a slanting board onto a tabletop. A set of faces would be selected by the experimenter and told to the subject so that the subject would have to concentrate on causing these faces to turn up by PK instead of unconsciously predicting them. In this way, the subject's possible ability to use precognition would be thrown out the window. Just to be sure, the scheduled faces would be changed periodically. And each face was selected as a target in the same number of tosses as the other faces.

Still the results indicated that there are people who have PK ability, since precognition was not a factor and the dice were named more accurately than mere chance guesses.

The best way to test for PK ability is to use moving objects such as dice. And work has been done with clocks, pendulums, flowing sand, and running water.

But what about living targets? You have heard stories about people who were able to influence animal behavior. There are those who claim that they can settle down wild horses by talking to them or blowing in their nostrils. And others are said to have a green thumb. Are they able to influence plant growth? Still others are said to be able to heal the sick without touching them.

Then there is the PK effect on stationary objects. Everyone has heard of tables being tipped in a séance. And there are stories about poltergeists, or unfriendly spirits, hurling dishes through the air. Could there be a connection between this and PK? Perhaps the events are people-made, not spirit-made.

Let's take the case of the Hermann family of Seaford, New York. In 1958, Mr. and Mrs. James M. Hermann and their two children, James and Lucille, went through a bad five weeks. From February 3 to March 10, strange things happened. A figurine flew through the air toward the TV set. A bottle of ink sailed through the air, went through the doorway, and spilled on the rug in the next room. A sixteen-inch-high plaster statue of the Virgin Mary leaped from one dresser to another. A bottle of shampoo moved across the bathroom shelf. There were sixty-seven of these incidents that happened during those five awful weeks.

Hermann had called the police, of course. But while detective Joseph Tozzi was talking to members of the family, things started sailing through the air. It was time for J. Gaither Pratt, of the Duke laboratory, to move in.

He felt that fifty of the sixty-seven happenings could be ignored, since it was possible that they had been done by trickery. After he had narrowed the field down to seventeen occurrences, he began his work.

It was found that nothing moved in the house when it

was empty. But when things began flying about, it was most often James who was around somewhere.

Pratt pointed out that he could find no evidence of trickery. And he was in the house when five of the flights took place. Pratt said that unconscious PK is very often found in cases where a person who is approaching adolescence is nearby.

One of the most amazing new stars of PK is Uri Geller. He is a young Israeli who seems to have a great deal of ability in using PK. In 1971, it was found that he could break a gold ring held in another person's clenched fist — solely by concentration. He could start broken clocks and watches without touching them. He could move watch hands forward or backward by concentration.

When Geller bent a ring that belonged to Dr. Friedbert Karger of the Max Planck Institute in Berlin, Germany, it was suggested that he might be using a concealed laser beam. Karger said that this was nonsense. "I never took my eyes off the ring or let it out of my hand. Geller only touched it lightly with his fingers. For the moment, one cannot say anything regarding the energy he uses."

When Geller met with Dr. Wernher von Braun, who was with the National Aeronautics and Space Administration (NASA) at the time, von Braun's electric calculator refused to function when the Israeli was in the room. This also happened when Uri came to the Stanford Research Institute in California to be tested.

Two physicists there were to do the testing. They were Dr. Harold Puthoff, a quantum and laser physicist, and Dr. Russell Targ, a plasma and laser physicist.

All of the materials in their tests were new to Uri. He had not supplied any of them. All of the sessions were either filmed or videotaped to find out if the observers had been hypnotized. In one experiment, Geller was able to unbalance a precision scientific scale that had been placed inside a large bell jar. He bent a steel band to an angle that would have required one hundred pounds of applied pressure — without touching the band.

Then ten film cans were lined up, with an object inside

only one of them. Uri passed his hands over the cans and named the one with the object inside. The cans were shifted, the object was put in another can, and Geller located it again. This happened twelve straight times without a miss. The odds? One in a trillion.

In 1973, Geller made some show business appearances. Appearing on a Jack Paar TV show, he had Paar hold a nail. Uri lightly stroked the end of the nail and it bent. Paar was shaken by this and left the stage before the show was over.

On a BBC television show in England, Geller sketched a copy of a drawing that had been made by a member of the crew and had been sealed in an envelope. He bent and broke kitchen forks. He made watches start ticking. All of this was done in the presence of two scientists. Later the station received calls from viewers of the show. They said that forks in their own houses had also been bent during the program.

There are those who believe and those who don't. Uri Geller is a controversial person. But so far, neither scientists nor magicians have been able to prove that he is a fraud.

Human beings may not be the only ones to have some PK abilities. In one experiment, cockroaches were placed in cages that were electrically wired.

A coin was flipped on a grid by an automatic flipper. If the coin landed on heads, a circuit was completed and the cockroaches would be shocked. If it landed on tails, the circuit was not completed and the insects would not be shocked.

Out of sixty thousand trials, the cockroaches were shocked more than 51 percent of the time. This is better than the 50 percent you might expect. But you also might wonder. If the cockroaches were able to influence the coin flip with psychokinesis, why did they choose to be shocked?

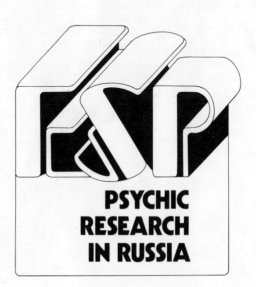

**PSYCHIC
RESEARCH
IN RUSSIA**

Russian scientists seem to be more concerned with psi experimentation than scientists of any other country. A lot of work is going on there.

In 1972, Stanley Krippner and Richard Davidson of the Maimonides Institute went to the USSR. They met Edward Naumov who directs the Institute of Technical Parapsychology at the City of Moscow Engineering Institute. He is also a member of the physics department there, and he was the host for the visiting Americans.

Krippner and Davidson described some of the work going on in Russia. In the United States and other Western countries, research is planned so that it will prove the existence of ESP and PK. In the Soviet Union, it is not usually done this way. Researchers are more interested in looking for practical applications of psi, since they feel that the existence of ESP and PK has already been established.

The Soviet government supports their research. And instead of referring to ESP as extrasensory perception, they call it biological information. Clairvoyance is called bio-location, and they are spending a lot of time studying dowsing and skin vision. For example, some people have been found who can tell the color of a card while blindfolded, merely by feeling it.

Further, the Russians break PK into two divisions — spontaneous and experimental. Spontaneous psychokinesis happens when objects move for no apparent reason. Experimental psychokinesis occurs when things are moved on purpose by someone who is trying to move them with PK.

There is also a lot of concern over what they call bioplasmic energy. This is an energy that the Russians claim seems to flow from the acupuncture points on the human body, but it is also found in plants. There is a woman, Nina Kulagina, who is especially good at PK. While she is performing her feats, her weight is reported to go down and her blood sugar level rises. Also, it is said, her bioplasmic field extends all over her body in an aura and pulsates in a rhythm.

The Russians believe that this bioplasmic energy can be photographed. The technique for photographing this energy was invented by Semyon and Valentina Kirlian in Russia. An electric Tesla coil (a type of transformer) is connected to two plates. A living or nonliving object is placed between the plates. A piece of film touches the object. When a switch is turned on, a high energy frequency is generated that causes the film to record an "aura." No camera is used.

Zakir Hussein is a musician who plays a small Indian hand drum. He had his fingertips photographed by Kirlian photography before a concert. There were heavy red blotches surrounding the tips of his fingers. These were not on the fingers themselves, but rather in the air around the tips. These auras looked like little halos. After the concert, the Kirlian process was repeated. This time there were red, white, and blue streamers coming out of the fingertips.

The experimenters say that the blotchy red halos show an anxious state of mind. The more relaxed people are, the bigger the glow on the photos. If this technique is perfected, it could possibly be used in the diagnosis of people with mental disorders. It would be of great value to biologists, physicians, and psychiatrists.

And it seems to work with plants. When pictures of plants were taken, it was found that there is a more intense aura around the bud and flower areas. That is where a lot of the biological action is taking place. Leaves are also high producers. But the auras get more intense when the bud or flower is cut off the plant. Streams of light come out of the wounds. Then they get weaker and weaker and disappear when the bud or flower dies.

Kirlian photography is becoming popular in the United States, too. Not only is it being studied by adults at such places as the Maimonides, but also teen-age scientists are becoming more interested in it. At the 1974 National Science Fair, there were two young high school physicists who had won their state science fair championships. And both of them had built their own Kirlian photography equipment.

The future developments in PK and ESP research will be something to see.

**PRO
OR CON?**

A man is walking on the deck of a ship. He suddenly has an uncontrollable urge to open a certain door to a certain cabin. When he does, he finds a man about to hang himself. A life is saved.

A woman is many miles away from her husband. But she hears him calling her. She drives to the zoo where he works as a snake keeper. There he is on the floor, repeating her name. He has been bitten by a cobra. Antivenin is administered. Another life is saved.

Do you believe these stories? Some people would say that they illustrate amazing coincidences. Others would feel that some people have psychic power and there is a scientific explanation for the happenings.

The anti-ESP group says that ESP research overlooks errors, uses prejudiced witnesses, and comes up with weak theories. They say that researchers are biased and do not carry on true scientific experimentation.

The pro-ESP group admits that a lot of work has to be done. However, much is already known about extrasensory perception. And just because we can't take a picture of it doesn't mean that it doesn't exist.

As J. B. Rhine has said: "Among the scientific professions of the Western world, there has grown up a conviction that the universe is physical, and that anything that does not fit the physical picture is unreal and should be ignored if it cannot be disproved. . . . The natural result is a silent boycott of any unassimilable claim that arises, and this is the real opposition parapsychology has now to encounter."

But neither side seems to realize that they have been getting closer and closer together in the last one hundred years. When ESP was first being examined back in the 1880s, there was no television or radio. Most people had only the Morse telegraph to send messages to each other. Houses were lit by gas lamps or oil lamps. There were no airplanes and few automobiles. People had never heard of X rays. The discoverers of DNA and RNA had not even been born. No wonder early ESP research looked like witchcraft. Even hypnotists were suspected of being fakes.

Since those days we have learned a lot that might have seemed to be black magic one hundred years ago. We know that there are other ways of receiving messages than just by our five most common senses. Bats have a sort of built-in radar system. Other animals can detect electrical charges that we cannot feel and infrared light that we cannot see. We know that the weather affects human behavior through the nervous system and the blood stream. We know that certain body odors that we are not aware of smelling can affect our opinions of other people.

There are countless other senses that were not even suspected in the 1880s. And probably many more that we do not know of today. Maybe there is no such thing as *extra*sensory perception. That is, maybe there are no outside senses, just senses that we have not discovered yet.

Let's keep an open mind.

The study of ESP is a young one. Scientists have been looking at the stars, studying plants and animals, experimenting with chemicals, and improving cattle and crops for centuries.

But there are some things to be considered in the future. First, we have to have much more information about ESP. Thousands, even millions, of cases must be studied. We have to find out more about why certain people seem to have the knack more than others. We have to find out if people can be trained to improve their abilities.

The big problem is to overcome prejudice. Just because ESP cannot be defined exactly and many of the ESP experiments cannot be repeated exactly is no reason to reject it completely. It wasn't too long ago that people rejected the germ theory of disease just because they had never seen bacteria.

And some people reject certain parts of ESP just because they don't want to believe in it. That is similar to the uneducated person who was taken to the zoo for the first time. He saw his first elephant and said, "There ain't no such animal."

But hold on to your hats. If the day ever comes when we all believe in psi, what will happen? If it is proved that some people can cause objects to move by psychokinesis, what happens to our ideas about the laws of motion in physics? If it is proved that ideas can be sent or received by clairvoyance and telepathy, what happens to our ideas about how the brain operates biologically? If it is proved that some people can predict the future through precognition, what happens to our ideas about the passage of time and the speed of light in astronomy?

That's enough to frighten almost anybody. Perhaps every one of us will have to start school all over again.

Clairvoyance: The extrasensory perception of events that are taking place at the time of the perception.

EEG: Abbreviation for the electroencephalogram produced by an electroencephalograph.

Electroencephalograph: A machine for detecting and recording brain waves. It can also be used to monitor the activity of the brain during sleep.

ESP: See extrasensory perception.

Extrasensory perception: A part of the science of parapsychology. It contains the phenomena of clairvoyance, precognition, and telepathy, but does not include psychokinesis. It is also referred to as ESP.

Parapsychology: The science of the study of clairvoyance, precognition, telepathy, and psychokinesis. It is also referred to as psychical research, or psi.

PK: See psychokinesis.

GLOSSARY

Poltergeist: From the German, meaning a noisy or rattling spirit. Mediums and spiritualists consider it to be the ghost of a dead person that delights in moving objects around.

Precognition: The extrasensory perception of events in the future.

Psi: See parapsychology.

Psychical research: See parapsychology.

Psychokinesis: A part of the science of parapsychology. It is the movement of objects by means of mind power — without touching the objects. It is also referred to as PK.

Psychometry: A type of telepathy in which an object such as a picture is read, rather than the thoughts of a person. The sender is nonliving instead of living. It is also referred to as psychoscopy.

Psychoscopy: See psychometry.

Rapid eye movements: Darting movements of the eye, common during periods of dreaming, similar to the eye movements used while watching films or television. They are also referred to as REM's.

REM's: See rapid eye movements.

Retrocognition: The extrasensory perception of past events.

Telekinesis: Psychokinesis. The word is no longer in use.

Telepathy: The extrasensory perception of someone else's mental state.

Zener cards: A deck of twenty-five cards used in ESP experimentation. The cards are marked with crosses, circles, stars, squares, and wavy lines. Each of these "suits" contains five cards.

Agee, Doris. *Edgar Cayce on ESP*. New York: Hawthorn Books, Inc., 1969.

Brown, Beth. *E.S.P. with Plants and Animals*. New York: Simon and Schuster, Inc., 1971.

Cohen, David. *ESP: The Search Beyond the Senses*. New York: Harcourt Brace Jovanovich, 1973.

Klein, Aaron E. *Beyond Time and Matter: A Sensory Look at ESP*. Garden City, New York: Doubleday & Company, Inc., 1973.

Knight, David C., ed. *The ESP Reader*. New York: Grosset & Dunlap, Inc., 1969.

Rhine, J. B., and Brier, Robert, eds. *Parapsychology Today*. New York: The Citadel Press, 1968.

Watson, Lyall. *Supernature*. Garden City, New York: Doubleday & Company, Inc., 1973.

BIBLIOGRAPHY

INDEX

Thomas Aylesworth holds a Ph.D. from Ohio State University. He has taught science at the university level, and he has worked for many years as a science editor and author. He belongs to numerous professional organizations; sails; plays tennis; and enjoys music. Dr. Aylesworth and his family live in Stamford, Connecticut.

**ABOUT
THE AUTHOR**